LIVING ROOMS

LIVING ROOMS

·····································

A PRACTICAL GUIDE TO DESIGN AND DECOR

MEREHURST

EMMA SCATTERGOOD

First published in 1997 by Merehurst Limited,
Ferry House, 51-57 Lacy Road, Putney, London SW15 1PR

Copyright © Merehurst Limited 1997

Handback ISBN 1 85391 5149
Paperback ISBN 185391 6137

A catalogue record of this book is available from
the British Library

Edited by Cally Law
Designed by Sue Miller
Special photography by Tim Imrie
Styled by Clare Louise Hunt
Illustrated by Susie Morris/Brihton Illustration

Colour separation by P&W Graphics Ltd
Printed in Italy by Olivotto

ACKNOWLEDGEMENTS
The publisher would like to thank the following photographers and
organisations for their permission to reproduce the photographs listed:

ABODE: page 31 — Ian Parry
CAMERA PRESS: pages 4, 23 & 55 — Schöner Wohnen; page 21— Bo
Appeltofft, page 25 — James Merrell; page 43 — Living
ELIZABETH WHITING & ASSOCIATES: page 33 — Michael Dunn;
page 35 — Nedra Westwater
INTERNATIONAL INTERIORS: pages 4, 9, 14 & 31 — Paul Ryan
ROBERT HARDING SYNDICATION: pages 2, 21, 27 & 29 — Russel Sadur;
pages 3 & 13 — Jan Baldwin; page 7 — Tim Imrie;
pages 11, 16 & 35 — James Merrell; pages 19 & 28 — Dominic
Blackmore; page 39 — Graham Rae; pages 52 & 53 — Rapid Eye

Contents

Introduction

Of all the rooms in the house, the living room works the hardest. While a few houses may boast drawing rooms, studies and libraries, most of us are lucky to have both a separate lounge and dining room. The living room has become the centre of our lives. It is the place where we entertain, relax, watch television, pursue our hobbies and read.

It is also the room that is most 'on view'. Your living room presents visitors — whether you like it or not — with an instant impression of your home and the sort of person you are, of your sense of style and your individuality.

So how do you go about creating a room that is practical and stylish, yet gives just the impression you want? And, more importantly, how can you do it on a shoestring budget? It is easy (but boring) to create an up-to-the-minute living room if you can afford to chuck out everything and start again, but most of us have to try and work miracles with an old three-piece suite and a grotty patterned carpet.

This book will show how all of this is possible. It will demonstrate how just one pot of paint really can transform a room and how to make the most of what you have got — including things you thought were fit only for the bin. It will show you how to use colour, light and accessories in stylish and inventive ways and, most important of all, it will teach you how to gain that one crucial thing — confidence.

Most of us have an idea of the sort of effect we would like to achieve but are not sure how to set about it. With confidence in your own ideas and in your ability to put them into practice, you will find that you make less mistakes — and have a lot more fun. The following pages are full of practical advice and inspirational pictures to give you all the confidence you need.

Happy decorating!

Right: You don't need a lot of money to create an impressive room. Confidence with colour and a little imagination are all that are required.

Chapter one
Be functional

I f you are serious about creating a wonderful living room you need to go about it in a serious manner. That is not to say the project won't be fun — it will be — but you will also save time and money if you approach the redesign of your front room as a professional would.

Any interior designer worth their salt would start by spending a substantial amount of time discussing your living room and how it is used before they so much as glanced at a colour card. Of course you want the room to look great — but you need it to be practical too. Professional designers refer to this first crucial stage as 'taking the brief' — when they arrive at your home armed with notebook and tape measure to take detailed notes about the room, what it is used for and what you hope to get out of it.

Why not sit down, take a long look at your room and take your own brief? You can ask other members of the family for their input at this stage too — that way you can be sure that everyone's expectations are met, at least to some extent.

This approach may seem excessive if you were planning only to slap on some fresh paint and rearrange the furniture, but it will really help you to get the best out of your room.

Taking the brief: Likes/dislikes

When you walk into your living room, which things immediately strike you as good or bad features? Make a note of these now — even if you are not sure yet how you would set about improving on them. It will help if you can remember what you loved or hated about the room on the day you moved in. First impressions count, but as time passes you can get used to the most frightful things and the true horror can fade in front of your eyes.

A good design is one that is well balanced — in other words, no one thing in a room should strike you the moment you walk through the door. Each element of the room should complement the other elements. Visitors should walk into your room and comment on how attractive the whole room is, not just the wallpaper or carpet.

Do not despair if your list of 'hates' is twice the length of your list of 'likes'. Later you will see how plenty of problems need not be problems at all — or can be disguised at least. Sometimes even the most unfortunate of features can be transformed into something characterful, if not beautiful!

Is the room light or dark?

If your living room doesn't get much natural light you will need to bear that in mind when it comes to choosing your colour scheme. It is usual to want to create as much of an

8

impression of light in a room as possible, although if you feel you are fighting a losing battle, you may consider emphasizing a room's darker, more dramatic nature. Perhaps you work long hours and only use your living room when it is dark anyway, in which case a shortage of natural light is not a problem.

Also think about how you might improve upon the light in the room. If your budget will extend to it, you may want to consider adding another window — or perhaps you could replace a solid door with a glazed one. These are decisions that should be made at the planning stage — not once the wallpaper is up on the walls!

If the room is naturally light you will have more of an open hand when it comes to decorating. However, it may be that you have large windows that dominate the room and you need to direct the focus of the room elsewhere.

Which way does the room face?
This will affect the light that a room receives. A room that faces north, east or northeast will usually receive a colder light than one that faces south, west or southwest, and so will need a warmer colour scheme to make it feel more comfortable (see Colour, page 16).

How do you use your living room?
Consider what you do in your living room and what should be incorporated into your new-look room to make it practical as well as stylish.

The following questions may point you in the right direction:

Who will be using the living room?
Is it a place where people read or do particular hobbies and will they need special seating, tables or lighting?

Do you watch television here?
The set will need to be positioned appropriately, bearing in mind how light reflects off the screen and where the chairs are.

Will your hi-fi be in this room?
You may want to consider a storage unit for the hi-fi. If so, you should check that there are enough power points for both this and the TV.

Do you need somewhere for drinks?

Is there sufficient heating?
Will you want to install a fire or radiators? You may like to consider a dummy fireplace simply to provide a focus to the living room.

Is the lighting adequate?
Does one person like to read while another watches TV, works or dozes? You may need different types of lighting around the room and plenty of power points (see Lighting, page 30).

Do you need more storage for books?
Consider where you could put this and if you want your books on view or hidden away.

Do you have personal collections you would like to display?
You will need shelf space and maybe appropriate lighting to show them off.

Does the living room also serve as a dining room?
Think about creating a special dining area. Perhaps it could have a different floor covering, be cut off by a screen and given subdued lighting.

What is your budget?
One of the most crucial parts of the brief. Before you head for the DIY store, it is important that you fix a top figure, setting aside about 10 per cent for any unforeseen expenditures — there are sure to be some once work begins.

Then it is up to you to juggle the budget according to your own

priorities. If you simply must have a luxurious wool carpet, that's fine, but it may mean you have to opt for cheaper wallpaper and lighting. Take another look at your personal brief and decide which of your planned changes are the most important to you.

Once you start your research into furniture and furnishings,

keep a note of the projected cost of each item, then add it all up before you spend a penny. That way you can be sure that you keep within your means.

Why not keep a smart notebook or folder for all your plans? It will be a useful reference if you need to check any details in the future and an interesting memento in years to come.

Above: A collection of plates attractively arranged gives this room its personality.

11

Chapter two

Making the most of what you've got

Few people are lucky enough to be able to start from scratch each time they decorate. The majority have to make the most of existing carpets, worn curtains and sofas which have seen better days. We also have to live with the existing structure of the house — whether we like it or not. There is only so much knocking down of walls, lowering of ceilings and extending into the garden that one house can take — and when you are working to a budget, drastic changes such as these are likely to be curtailed by monetary factors.

Do not despair. Your living room can be transformed with just a few clever decorating tricks — and none of them costs a fortune or requires building work. In fact, many living rooms with 'problem' features eventually become the most pleasing rooms of all.

Coping with existing furnishings

While taking your brief you will have listed the things that bother you most about your living room as it stands. You will also have begun to work out your budget, which will give you an idea of what you can afford to replace and what you will have to live with for another few years. Again, it is up to you to juggle your priorities. If opting for paint rather than wallpaper means you can afford to ditch the awful carpet, then go for it!

Do a bit of research before you start and you may find that you can do some things for less money than you anticipated. You might find a carpet remnant that fits your living room perfectly (especially if it is a small room), or you may spot a special offer on the ideal wallpaper. You never know, miracles sometimes happen...

Inevitably, however, there will be several things that you have to put up with for a few more years. Here's how to make the most of them:

The old sofa

Having an old sofa or armchair re-upholstered can sometimes cost as much as buying a new one, so unless the sofa is of a reasonable quality and you are happy with the shape and size of it, it is probably not worth considering. What might be worthwhile, however, is finding someone to make loose covers. These are a cheaper option and can be taken off for washing and even changed to suit the seasons. Some companies offer washable elasticated covers which, with a bit of fiddling, will look as if they were made to fit your sofa.

If you want to spend as little money as possible on revamping your settee, try covering it with plenty of large scatter cushions artfully placed to hide the worn patches. Or give it a completely new look by covering it with a throw. You have to accept that the look will be casual rather than tailored, but for cost-effectiveness and practicality it can't be beaten. Plenty of shops now stock a good range of throw-overs, but you can get something unique — and a better fit

Right: You can give old furniture a new lease of life without spending a fortune.

Above: The impression of space has been maximized in this room by keeping the level of the furniture low, allowing the eye to pass over it to the far sides of the room.

— if you make it yourself. It is easy to do and gives you the chance to mix-and-match more successfully with other soft furnishings in the room. Turn to page 60 for instructions on how to make a customized throw.

The dreadful carpet

Your living room is likely to be a high-traffic area — being used for entertaining and relaxing more than any other room in the house — so you need flooring that can take the strain.

Carpet remains one of the largest investments you will have to make, so it can be depressing to be faced with an existing carpet that is either falling to pieces or so ugly it makes you fall apart yourself every time you catch sight of it. Ripping it up is not your only option however.

If the problem is simply a few bare patches, you could arrange your furniture to cover the worst of them and invest in a strategically placed rug or two. If the whole carpet is beyond hope, you could buy a cheap rug large enough to cover the majority of it and then artfully site

your furniture over the surrounding area.

Check the state of the floor beneath your carpet. You may be lucky and discover some perfect floorboards or parquet just waiting to be renovated. Bare varnished boards can look really smart as well as being hardwearing and cheap (see Flooring, page 32).

An ugly fireplace

Old gas fires can be particularly unattractive, so, unless yours is in constant use, consider ways of concealing it — perhaps with a folding screen or a light piece of furniture. If it is not often used, why not take it out completely? Pretty Victorian fireplaces are often reasonably priced at architectural salvage yards and they can be installed very cheaply if you don't necessarily want to light a fire in them.

Shabby furniture

It is amazing how you can transform a plain shabby piece of furniture with just a little time and attention. So long as the basic shape is appealing, it is easy to turn it into something special. Look at your old tables and chests of drawers. Could the handles or feet be changed? How would they look if the paint or varnish were stripped off and restored? Perhaps they would look great painted or stencilled to match your colour scheme.

(Turn to page 54 for instructions on how to distress a painted chest.) It is well worth experimenting — after all, what have you got to lose?

Coping with structural problems

Even the most perfect houses have their shortcomings, although many of them are subject to individual taste: one person's 'cramped' is another person's 'cosy', for instance. You may not be able to change the structure of your living room, but you can alter the impression the room gives by emphasizing certain aspects and concealing others. Here are some of the most common problems and how to rectify them:

Ceilings

People tend to lose interest when it comes to ceilings. They spend ages deliberating over walls, floors and furniture — then simply slap white emulsion above it all. That's fair enough, but using colour on the ceiling can help you create the look you are after. (Turn to page 16 for more tips on colour.)

Making it lower

A living room should be a cosy, welcoming space. If your living room feels rather cold and unfriendly because the ceiling is too high, try to emphasize the ceiling space in some way to make it appear to advance towards you and become lower. Paint it a darker, warmer colour than the walls or, if you are feeling bold, use a patterned paper, such as Anaglypta. Add a picture rail and extend the ceiling colour down to the rail for extra effect, and perhaps decorate the walls in horizontal stripes.

Making it higher

Modern houses with their lower ceilings usually have the opposite problem. In this instance, there is an argument for using white paint as it will make the ceilings recede from view.

White is rather uninteresting for a living room, however, so why not be a bit more adventurous? You can achieve the same receding effect by painting the ceilings in a cool colour, such as a pastel shade, lighter than the walls below.

You can also use pattern to achieve the effect you want. Painted vertical stripes or a vertically striped wallpaper will accentuate the height of the walls and appear to lift the ceiling up.

Making the living room larger

Most people feel that they have not got enough space, but you can fool the eye into thinking that a room is larger than it is by playing with the scale of the furniture in the room. If you are replacing furniture, opt for smaller and lower pieces, such as neat two-seater sofas, little wicker armchairs and tiny coffee tables that do not overpower the room or obscure the far reaches.

Emphasize the width of the room with shallow, wide pieces placed along the walls and choose fitted carpet, which naturally draws the eye to the corners. Pick light colours for your decoration and furnishings and avoid anything but the smallest of patterns, particularly on walls.

Making the living room wider

If you have a knock-through living room where two adjacent rooms have been converted into one, it can easily adopt the appearance of a tunnel — especially if there are only two windows, one at each end. You should aim to draw those two ends of the room inwards and break up the stretch of floorway running between them.

Choose warm, bold colours for the ends of the room, especially for the curtains, which when drawn will bring the room 'together' more. Most importantly, avoid placing all your furniture along the walls. Try to break up the room by placing two small sofas opposite each other, one in the middle of the room, or by using small tables to create islands of interest.

Chapter three

Colour

Ask people what confuses them most when it comes to designing their homes and the answer is likely to be colour. Deciding on a colour scheme, choosing which colours go with which and then putting together fabric and wallpaper samples usually has the effect of sending most people back to square one and a pot of magnolia. In years gone by, this wasn't such a problem, but current trends are encouraging us to be bold and to dip our brushes into indigo blues, sunflower yellows and even tangerines. So where do you start and how can you gain the confidence to put together the living room of your dreams?

The first step is to learn a little theory. It may sound boring and a long way from the immediate problem of matching your curtains to your sofa, but once you understand how colours 'work', the decisions will be much easier to make.

The colour wheel

Interior designers often refer to a 'colour wheel' — a basic way of demonstrating how certain colours mix together to make other colours (red and blue produce purple, for example). The wheel can be divided into halves — one half comprising the warm colours (red, red/orange, orange, yellow/orange and yellow and their various tints and shades) and the other the cool colours (green, blue/green, blue and blue/violet and their tints and shades).

The warm colours are also known as 'advancing' colours, as they tend to make walls look closer to you. Cool colours on the other hand, are referred to as 'receding', as they have the effect of moving away from you.

Choosing a colour

Using this basic theory you can create a living room that looks

Right: Proof that neutrals needn't be boring: this room has been decorated with as much emphasis on texture as colour.

either bigger or smaller than it really is, lighter or darker and either warmer or cool and airy.

Remember that the darker shades of any colour, including green and blue, will make your living room look smaller than a pastel shade. Try not to let the size of your living room put you off the warmer or darker shades completely, however. A small room that gets enough light can look quite stunning in a rich orange or deep green — especially if you tend to use the room more often in the evening, subtly lit by artificial light.

Think about the kind of effect you want to achieve. For traditional impact go for a deep red or library green, for modern chic opt for mauves, lime greens and even orange. Or perhaps you would prefer something more subtle, such as a pastel pink or mint.

Different colours have been proven to have certain psychological effects. If you see your living room as a retreat, somewhere to relax and be yourself, then go for blue, the colour of harmony and peace. If you want a living room that livens you up each morning, try yellow — a joyful, sunny colour associated with creative energy and power. If you fancy something more traditionally warm, you could go for red. But be

warned, red is an appetite-inducing colour!

Although some colour schemes use just one colour and then accessorize it with various shades of the same hue, most tend to pick out an accent colour from the opposite side of the colour wheel to add a dash of interest.

If you choose a mainly blue living room, add a few yellow cushions to your sofa and pick out some yellow or orange in the curtaining or on a vase for extra sparkle. If you fancy dramatic red walls, try going for lampshades in an equally deep shade of green. A living room offers plenty of opportunity for adding flashes of contrasting colour in cushions, rugs and lampshades — as well as more obvious statements in the larger pieces, such as the sofa, carpet and curtains.

If the concept of decorating in red and green or bright blue and yellow is still rather hard for you to handle, turn to nature for proof of success. Think of a bright-blue iris, its centre shot with yellow, or a deep-green holly bush laden with red berries. Nature never gets it wrong and can be a great source of inspiration. Perhaps your living room opens up or looks out on to the garden? If so, let the colours of the shrubs or perhaps the spring flowers play their part in your decision-making.

Using existing furnishings for inspiration

If you are still stuck for ideas or confused about where to start, existing furnishings that need to be incorporated into the scheme may help rather than hinder.

If your sofa has to stay put, decide whether you would like it to play a large or minor part in the colour scheme. If you would rather play it down, take your main colour from the opposite side of the colour wheel and use the sofa merely as an accent. If you decide to use it as the major colour in the room, then look for paint or wallpaper in a similar shade and select an accent colour — or two — from the opposite side of the colour wheel. Consider yourself lucky if your existing curtains or sofa incorporate several different colours, as your colour scheming has already been done for you. Pick out one hue as your main colour and use the others to complement it around the room.

Using colour for definition

A living room tends by its very nature to be the focus of a range of different activities, from studying to relaxing or dining. Indeed, as the pressure on housing space grows and more people live in studio-style apartments, the demands put on this one room are increasing.

Right: Be as bold as you dare. Once you have gained colour confidence, stylish and stimulating schemes could transform your home.

Use colour and pattern to emphasize the various functions of the room and give different areas an appropriate look.

In a lounge/diner try decorating the dining area of the room in a different colour — or in the same shade as the sitting areas, but using a different pattern. An alcove, complete with desk and bookshelves, can become a designated study area simply by giving it a different splash of colour.

Natural living

If your furniture and accessories are largely wooden or made from stripped, natural materials, you may choose a neutral scheme to complement them. The key here is to introduce a range of shades to add interest. Going for a neutral living room doesn't mean everything has to be white.

Extend the range of colours in your furnishings to cream,

ochre, coffee — and maybe shades of grey. Black is a neutral colour, but it can be harsh and should be used sparingly.

These neutral shades, especially white and black, can be used in most colour schemes as an extra accent colour. See how a black cast-iron fireplace sits well in any scheme, as does white woodwork.

Pattern and texture

A living room with a neutral colour scheme relies on pattern and texture for extra interest. A natural room will never be boring if sisal flooring is combined with textured rugs, muslin at the window, silk cushions and a roughly hewn wooden coffee table. Use pattern and texture to enhance any colour scheme, however bright and bold.

Chapter four

Themes

Giving your living room a theme adds interest and cohesion to your design and can actually make the decision process easier. You may not want a living room to be as obviously themed as a bathroom perhaps, but you can still create a certain style. It needn't be complicated — you could take something as simple as a colour to be your inspiration.

Starting points

Gather your thoughts and focus your mind by looking through books and magazines for inspiration. Study the pictures of living rooms that appeal to you and ask yourself why you like them. Is it the colour combination, the way the furniture has been arranged, the window dressing or the style and design of the furnishings?

You may not be able to buy the exact pieces of furniture shown, but you can take inspiration from the overall look. Try collating a scrapbook of pictures that appeal to you. As time goes by, you may notice the same styles and themes appearing time and time again as your preferences become clearer.

A bit of history

The advantage of using historical references as your starting point is that they will never date — and with a bit of skill you can mix-and-match more contem-porary pieces into the scheme so that you never tire of it.

The age of your home may be inspiration enough. If it is Victorian or Edwardian, you could recreate a Victorian parlour in your living room — with floor-length curtains, walls in classic shades of red or green or perhaps a traditional patterned wallpaper, a fireplace as a focal point and small circular tables draped with pretty fabrics and lace. A Georgian living room would have been fresher, with eau de nil walls and less clutter. Or perhaps you have a cottage with dark wooden beams lending itself to Tudor-style tapestry fabrics, heavy wooden chairs and pewter accessories.

Rules are made to be broken of course, and simply because your house dates from 1930, there is no reason why you should not create the look of another era in your living room. Once you have lived in your new home for a while you will develop a stronger feel for what sort of design would be sympathetic to it.

Fashions and movements

Throughout history there have always been alternative movements in style — groups of people who have reacted against the mainstream designs of their time to produce something refreshingly different. The Arts and Crafts movement, epitomised by the work of William Morris, and the Shaker community of 19th-century America, which produced beautiful simple furniture, are just two to draw inspiration from. Leaf through design books to learn more about such styles — you may find one of them is just what you are looking for.

Further afield

Often a holiday abroad will inspire you to recreate the style of that country in your own front room. All cultures use colour in a different way, producing an exciting variety of schemes to draw from. White-washed walls combined with stunning blues and greens and washed wooden floors can look stunning, but remember that the light here is different to that of the Mediterranean and colours may not have the same vibrancy on a miserable day in Britain. Save such schemes for the sunniest of south-facing rooms.

Right: As much a theme as a colour scheme, blue and white looks both classic and chic.
Below right: A collection of ethnic treasures provided the starting point for this room.

Using what you have

There is no need to start from scratch — the inspiration for your theme could be sitting right under your nose. Oranges arranged in a bright blue bowl might give you the idea for a blue and orange living room, or a favourite rocking chair could direct you towards an American Colonial style.

If you have a collection to display then let it take centre stage and direct the colours and look of the rest of the room. The inspiration could even come from a small picture. The trick is to open your eyes to what you have around you and use what others have done before. You can cheat as much as you like!

Let it grow

Often the living room that looks most comfortable and attractive is the one that has developed over time. Think of how some hotel rooms look well-designed but soulless. It is the accumulation of your personal touches that make a room effective.

Chapter five

Choosing and using furniture

L iving room furniture needs to be as comfortable as it is practical — and it has to look good too. These are high demands, and it is worth taking time to plan and research thoroughly before buying.

Start by taking a good look at what you've got already and ascertain what else you need. By making sketches of each wall in your living room you will begin to get an idea of how you want the room to look, where your existing furniture should go and what else you want to buy — but you need to be practical too.

Go back to your initial brief and look at how the room is used. This will dictate the type of furniture you buy and where it is positioned in the room. If the television can only go in one particular corner, then the sofa will need to be placed appropriately. If you want to eat at the end of the living room which overlooks the garden, the armchairs will have to go at the other end. And you will soon run out of valuable wall space for bookshelves, storage units and pictures — especially if there is a door on one wall and a radiator on another.

Planning on paper

To juggle furniture without breaking your back, do the initial planning on paper. You may have already drawn a floor plan when you took the measurements for carpet and so on. If not, do so now by transferring your measurements on to squared paper using a scale that allows you to fit your plan on a sheet of A4 or A3 — 1:20 is normally sufficient. Mark on it where your power points are, where the radiator is, where the TV socket is, the direction the doors open and the position of the window.

Right: An attractive screen effectively separates a practical working area from a comfortable living room. You could use such a screen to create a separate dining area too.

Now measure up the pieces of furniture which are staying in the room. You do not need their heights, only the widths and depths (though you could keep a note of heights in case you need them later). Adapt these measurements to the same scale as the floor plan and cut them out of squared paper. Write on each one what it is, so you don't get confused. Using your plan, you can play around with the positioning of the furniture until you achieve the perfect compromise of style and practicality.

If you are planning to buy a new sofa or table and do not know how big it is going to be, leaf through a few catalogues. You'll soon get an idea of the average sizes of a two- or three-seater sofa and the sort of table you want, and you can use these sizes as rough guides.

Once you are happy with the plan, or even just a part of it, trace it complete with positioned furniture onto tracing paper and put it to one side. You may find you do several tracings, but then you can compare them to help you make your final decision.

Effective positioning

The way you place your furniture can alter the effect of the whole room, making it appear spacious or cluttered, traditional or quirky. While you move your furniture around your plan, think about how you can position it in a more interesting and imaginative way.

It is easy to slip into the habit of putting everything slap up against the wall, with perhaps a coffee table as the only exception, but if your room has the space — and especially if it's a lounge/diner — you can try to create little islands of interest to break it up. Sofas do not need to have their backs up against the wall: try bringing them into the middle of the room instead, positioning two either back to back or facing each other.

Chairs do not need to face the centre of the room either — group some around a small table to create an intimate area within the larger room. Use screens, chests and tables to break up expanses of floor and experiment with the positioning of desks — could they face into the room instead of to the wall? You may find that by breaking the rules you make more efficient use of your space.

Practical positioning

Practical comfort and safety should be remembered when you play with your plan — especially if you have children. You need a certain amount of space between each piece of furniture and between furniture and a wall in order to pass comfortably between them. Check that there is room to draw back a chair or to circle a table, that heads won't be banged on overhead shelves and that there will be no trailing flexes that people might trip over.

Choosing a sofa or armchair

Deciding on the fabric of your sofa or armchair is just part of the process of choosing the actual chair. The next decision concerns the style — although you may have considered what sort of look you want, think about the practicalities of the style as well.

Do you tend to relax on the sofa alone or with your partner and/or children? If the whole family tends to gather on a sofa, you'll need one large enough to cope — or would two small sofas be better than one large one? Do you tend to sit on it, or do you prefer to stretch out or curl up. If you like to lie down to relax, you'll need a design which is not only long enough, but which has comfortable armrests for your head or feet.

If one person likes to stretch out and another sit, you'll need one long sofa and one armchair. Does anyone in the family have a back problem or are there any elderly members of the family? If so, they won't appreciate a design which is hard to raise themselves out of. Check the comfort of a chair by sitting on it in the shop in the manner that you would at home. There is no point in resting your bottom on the seat for a few seconds, then jumping up and declaring it to be fine. Ignore curious onlookers and relax into the chair. The upholstery should support you without sagging or being too rigid. Are the small of your back and your neck comfortably supported, and are the arms of the chair at a good height?

If your house doesn't have a spare room, you may want to consider a sofabed, which is as comfortable as a normal sofa and makes a good occasional bed too. The cheaper models fold out to provide just a mattress on the floor, but most open out on to legs with a separate mattress.

The quality of the mattresses can vary considerably, along with the price, so consider carefully how often it will be used as a bed, compare the different types for comfort and then make your decision.

Above: Selecting just the right armchair or sofa will make all the difference to your living room.

Finally, don't feel you have to buy a three-piece suite — or indeed any matching upholstery. A living room looks more effective if the upholstery has been mixed and matched with different styles of chairs and sofa. Pick out one or two colours that complement your scheme and look out for patterns that incorporate one or both of them. Don't be nervous about combining checks and stripes, or even checks and florals. If the shades are right you'll be successful. All it takes is a little confidence in your colour skills.

Chapter six

Dressing your windows

The way you dress your windows will set the tone of your living room and indeed of the whole house — for curtains and blinds play a large part in how your home looks from the outside too.

Living room window dressings are important for both style and practicality — probably more so than in any other room of the house. If you use the living room during the day, you need to make the most of available light. Additionally, if you spend most evenings in your living room you will want a sense of warmth and privacy too. The best window dressings will offer all this — and look good at the same time.

Points to consider

There is a wealth of different styles to choose from, which makes the decision process harder than ever — but by focusing on your particular needs you can make it a little easier. Before you even begin to look at fabrics, consider the following points: your window type and what it overlooks, the style or theme of your living room and the amount of light the room receives.

The size and design of your windows will rule out certain designs immediately. Swags and tails sit less comfortably against modern picture windows, for example, while Venetian blinds do little for tiny cottage casements. Full-length curtains usually need taller windows in order to look balanced, and grand swags and rosettes require an equally imposing frame.

If your windows are small, or the living room doesn't get much light, full curtains and impressive pelmets may be unsuitable simply because they block out what light there is and make the room too dark. Go for simple designs without low pelmets and use tie-backs to open up the window area. Or you could extend your pole or track beyond the window frame so that the curtains do not obscure the glass at all.

Equally there could be a need to protect your room from strong daylight or unwelcome eyes — particularly if your furnishings might fade in the sun or you have valuables on display. In this case you will need to consider a combination of dressings, such as a flat blind and curtains.

Choosing a style:

Curtains
When drawn at night, curtains make a living room look cosy — and they help to keep it warm too, especially if they are given a thermal lining. Curtains finish and soften a window frame and provide added privacy in the evenings. However, because of the amount of fabric they use, they can add up to be a rather expensive option.

There is a vast selection of headings and styles available, from tab heads for a simple Shaker style, and the more conventional pencil pleats, right through to swags, tails, rosettes and shaped pelmets for traditional period living rooms Choose the finish to suit your room, or if that is beyond your means, consider a budget option from the following selection.

Right: Effective window dressings needn't be costly. Draping fabric from swag holders is an inexpensive yet stylish option.

Blinds

A cheaper option than curtains, blinds will minimize draughts and provide privacy. They also offer you more control over the amount of light you let into your living room. Roman, roller, paper and cane blinds roll or fold up to allow more light to enter when you need it, while slatted blinds can also be adjusted to allow more or less daylight to filter through the slats. All of these styles offer a simple minimalist effect but they can be dressed up with any of the finishes outlined below.

Festoon and Austrian blinds are more luxurious, with ruched fabric and frilled edges, but can be too fussy and 'feminine' for many living rooms.

Lace panels

Available ready-made in a variety of lengths, these allow light to filter attractively through the windows while offering privacy throughout the day — ideal if your living room is overlooked. A pretty alternative to conventional nets, they can be combined with curtains or a blind.

Shaped pelmets

Enjoying a well-deserved revival, the wooden pelmet is now available in an exciting range of designs which can be covered in fabric or painted to match your scheme. Combined with simple curtains it can be used to stun-

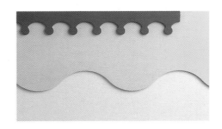

ning effect, but it also works well on a small window as a dressing in its own right. Take care over the size of your pelmet though and make sure it suits the scale of your window. See page 39 for details on how to make your own pelmet.

Dress curtains

If you never need to close your curtains — if they are combined with a blind or are framing a door to the garden for example — you needn't waste money on surplus fabric. Simply buy one width of fabric or enough to frame the sides of your window adequately. If the curtains are light enough, you may be able to dispense with conventional headings too by using a Velcro-type of tape: one length is sewn to your curtain and the other is stuck to the window surround, so you can simply 'stick' your curtains up.

Quick, cheap and easy

You do not need to spend a fortune or go for anything grand to dress your windows with style — some of the simplest ideas are often the best:

Left and right: Shaped pelmets can be made from MDF then painted or covered in fabric to complement your colour scheme.

Curtain clips

Just like normal curtain rings, but with a little clip at the bottom, these can be run along your pole in the usual way, then used for holding up pieces of fabric, muslin or lace — instant curtains with no sewing required. Curtain clips are ideal for minimalist living rooms or as a temporary measure.

Swag holders

These enable you to produce your own simple swagged pelmets without the formality or the cost of the real thing. All you have to do is feed a length of fabric through two of these curly metal brackets, fixed at either side of the top of your frame. The holders make it easy to create rosettes or let the fabric fall naturally so you can be as formal or relaxed as you please. Use them alone, over a blind or combined with curtains in a contrasting fabric.

Chapter seven
Living room lighting

You can spend months choosing fabrics, wallpaper and accessories, but if your lighting is ineffective your living room will lack atmosphere and warmth. One overhead light and a lamp in the corner are unlikely to be sufficient for any room, let alone one used for so many different activities.

Never underestimate the power of lighting. At the flick of a switch it can alter the mood, style and efficiency of your living room. The right lighting will transform a flat uninteresting room in which people strain their eyes into an instantly more welcoming place, spotlighting areas of interest and providing the right level of light for reading, sleeping, studying or watching television.

Planning your lighting

It is important that you plan your lighting before you start to think about decorating. Adapting lighting, putting in extra power points and fixing additional wall lights inevitably means fiddling with electrical wiring behind the plaster — and that means mess. You don't want to ruin your new paper just a week after it goes up.

Go back to your initial brief once more and think about what you and your family do in the living room. Do you like to read while someone else snoozes? If so, you will need good light, while they will prefer something more subdued. Do you use one end of the room as a formal dining area from time to time? It will need subtle romantic lighting to create the perfect mood. Do you have a good range of paintings or prints that you would like to illuminate? Or will your shelves be housing an interesting display of china?

Make a note to direct spotlights on to these points of interest, mount picture lights or add concealed lighting in your shelving. Whatever activities you indulge in, or mementos you treasure, planned lighting will make the living room a more pleasant place in which to enjoy them.

After you have planned the position of your furniture on your scaled paper plan, consider whether you have enough power points for additional lamps in the appropriate places. If the armchair you like to read in is going in one corner, check that there is space and a power point to put a reading light next to it. If there isn't, mark on your plan that you need a socket at that point. As a rule of thumb, you will need to have a lamp or light near or next to every seat in the room.

If you do use part of your living room as a dining area, treat that area separately and consider fitting another pendant light (perhaps with a dimmer switch) above the table. Or you could restrict your permanent fixtures to the sides of the room, perhaps in the form of wall lights or table lamps, and create a romantic atmosphere by lighting the table itself with candles.

Styles of lighting:

Ceiling lights
The most common light fittings of all, these are usually in the centre of the room and in the form of a pendant and shade, although there are plenty of other types of ceiling light to choose from. Think of the ceiling light as your starting point, then add extra lighting around the room. A pendant and shade will direct the light mostly downwards and outwards, according to the angle of the shade (although a lot of light is also lost through

the hole in the shade at the top, sending light up to the ceiling); spotlights allow you to direct light wherever it is needed; recessed downlighters shine a beam of light directly downwards; while domed ceiling fittings provide a diffused light.

Wall lights

These are a more subtle source of light than central ceiling fittings. Traditional bracket lamps with little shades are perfect for Victorian-style living rooms. Modern wall lights are often uplighters, sending light across the wall and up to the ceiling — so, although useful for adding attractive pools of light, they are not ideal for reading. Picture lights also come into this category and can be fitted above or below the object to be lit.

Table lamps

These can light the whole room or just small areas of it without the overhead glare of a central ceiling light. They also allow you to control which areas are lit. Position table lamps around the room to create warm pools of light and if possible arrange the wiring so that you can turn on all your table lamps at the flick of one central switch as soon as you walk into a room.

Floor lights

These are easy to move around the room, are useful for both general and specific lighting and

add new levels of light source. For positioning behind an armchair, look for a standard shade, for more general lighting go for an uplighter and for directed pools of light, choose a spotlight stand.

Candlelight

Don't keep candles purely for emergencies. They are a romantic and flexible light source, whether freestanding on a mantelpiece, wallmounted on a sconce or hung centrally on a chandelier or in a lantern. Soft and flattering, they create an atmosphere electric light will never match.

Top: A lamp at either end of a sofa not only balances the look, but provides adequate lighting for anyone wanting to read — wherever they choose to sit.

Above: A table lamp casts a soft glow over attractive gold painted lettering.

Chapter eight

Flooring

Choose the flooring for your living room to suit not only the room but also your lifestyle — and your budget. If the room is used regularly by a number of people and you have children or pets (or tend to be clumsy yourself) you will need a floor covering that can cope with the strain. If, however, you live alone and use the living room only to watch television or to entertain friends in the evenings, you may be able to get away with something more luxurious.

First you must decide whether you prefer hard flooring or carpet. A floor made of tiles, parquet or woodstrip will certainly be hardwearing as well as attractive. Wooden flooring is ideal for a traditional-looking living room, ranging from country or Shaker styles through to a simple Victorian look. Tiles are a more unusual (and costly) option for a living room, but can look cool and elegant or simple and rustic, depending on your choice of finish.

All hard flooring will take spills and act as a usefully neutral foil to your furniture and furnishings — and it will last for years, however many times you change your colour scheme. Hard floors are especially useful in living rooms that lead directly into the garden or on to the street. You will probably feel the need for a rug or two to soften the look, however, and that —

combined with the cost of wood or tiled flooring (plus underlay to stop rugs from slipping) — can be expensive.

Carpeting needs more maintenance — but it offers softness and warmth underfoot and a sense of wall-to-wall comfort. Its insulating qualities prevent footsteps from echoing around the house and, as there is such a wide range of materials and designs to choose from, there is sure to be one that suits your colour scheme and bank balance.

Don't forget to budget for underlay — a good underlay increases the life of a carpet, makes it softer to walk on and improves its insulating qualities. Foam-backed carpets are available as a cheaper alternative, but they are usually of inferior quality and their life span is accordingly much shorter.

If you are particularly worried about spills and damage, you could always try carpet tiles. These are made of heavy-duty materials and are easy to install and replace whenever necessary. The downside is that they are only available in a relatively limited range of colours.

When choosing your carpet, remember your colour theory in order to achieve the effect you are aiming for. Reds, oranges, and yellows will have a warming effect, while blues and greens will cool down the room. Plain light-coloured carpet fitted wall-to-wall will make a room appear larger, whereas a heavily patterned carpet in darker colours will have the opposite effect — though to a lesser extent. Plain carpet in either light or dark colours will show every stain and piece of fluff, whereas patterns will allow you to get away with more — ideal if you don't like housework. Take some carpet samples home to get a better impression of how they will look in your room.

There is a third flooring option which falls somewhere between soft and hard. Natural matting made from vegetable fibres such as sisal, coir, jute and seagrass is tough and hardwearing while offering some of the qualities of carpet — especially those varieties which combine natural fibres with the softness of wool and are laid over underlay. Natural flooring is generally available in neutral shades which complement any colour scheme (although coloured and patterned varieties are also on the market) and it suits traditional, rustic and more contemporary living rooms.

Before you decide one way or the other, lift the existing carpet and check what is underneath. You may be lucky enough to discover some forgotten parquet or decent floorboards lurking below. With a little sanding and a few coats of paint and/or varnish, you could have a beautifully restored hard floor for very little outlay. (Turn to page 56 for details on how to paint a stylish chequered floor.)

Before you rush off to hire your sander, however, do take up the carpet and check the complete floor — often you will find that a small area is beyond repair.

Right: A painted floor is a pretty yet hard-wearing option for a busy living room.

Chapter nine

Accessories

A living room without photographs, souvenirs or memorabilia of any kind is little more than a shell, however beautifully decorated it may be. Accessories form the heart and soul of a room, introducing personality, humour and interest.

There is an art to displaying your personal treasures — and choosing new ones to suit your redesigned living room — that ensures they earn the term 'accessory' and do not become simply 'clutter'.

Recognize a theme

If you have chosen a certain theme or style for your living room it will be easy to complement it with accessories in a similar vein. You could decorate the walls of a Victorian living room with traditional prints, photographs or paintings linked by a fabric bow. Finish a Shaker room with a peg rail hung with functional artefacts and some simple candle sconces. Enhance an ethnic setting with attractive rugs hung from wrought-iron curtain poles on the wall and perhaps a gilt-framed mirror. By turning to historical and geographical textbooks you will find a wealth of inspirational ideas.

It does not matter if you mix and match from across the years and oceans. Half the skill in decorating a home is in recognizing what will work together and what won't. Who cares if you put a Bakelite telephone in a Shaker-style room or a modern vase in a Georgian farmhouse? If you like it, do it — it's your home after all.

Out with the old?

Buying new accessories is all well and good, but what about your existing pieces? The strong-hearted may quote William Morris ('Have nothing in your houses that you do not know to be useful or believe to be beautiful') and refer half their ornaments to the bin. Indeed, unless you are an avid collector you may wonder if your treasures really are worth displaying. Think again. After all, you have spent some time amassing them.

Accessories do not have to be large or impressive to look the part, and even the simplest things gain credence and style once you have managed to arrange them successfully.

If you take a fresh look at your existing bits and pieces, you may begin to notice a common thread. Maybe you have several pots of the same house plant, or perhaps you have several different plants, all potted in the same style of earthenware. Perhaps you pick up a picture postcard every time you visit a gallery or shop and they are now dotted around the house, or you can't resist buying candles and candlesticks whenever one catches your eye.

By placing or hanging such things together they become a collection immediately and worth a second glance. It may be that the only link is colour, but that's fine. Position them together on a shelf or table, pin them on a peg board or group them on the wall. Next time you buy anything new, you will have a clearer idea of what will work and what won't.

Create a welcome

The most welcoming living rooms appeal to all the senses. Think about what you see, hear, smell and touch when you go into the room and choose accessories accordingly to create the perfect atmosphere. These little things have as much impact as the carpet or curtains.

Fresh flowers are a must for both visual appeal and scent. Don't worry if you can't arrange them — casual displays in the simplest vessel will still look and smell the part.

Candles are also essential — especially if you do not have the luxury of a real open fire. Positioned around the room to create soft pools of romantic light, candles are a quick and easy way of creating a welcome after dark. Make them work doubly hard for you and go for scented varieties — there is a wide range to choose from. Or put little night lights in an oil burner and heat fragranced essential oils. You don't even need a candlestick — a quick search around the house for alternatives such as terracotta pots, shallow dishes or baskets packed with moss will only increase the imaginative impact of your lighting.

Above, right and below: Displaying your collections, whether they are books, plates or hats, gives a living room a personal feel, while vases of fresh flowers make it more welcoming.

Stimulate the sense of touch with a pile of soft cushions, a chenille throw, a thick carpet to sink your toes into — and a warm radiator or fire.

And don't forget the sense of hearing. If you cannot guarantee pleasant birdsong immediately outside your window, use music to reflect or lift the mood.

Chapter ten

Putting your scheme together

You have decided on your living-room theme and colours — well almost, at least! The next stage is to finalise your choice of fabrics, paint, carpeting and so on by putting them all together. Don't feel daunted. If you take some tips from the professionals, you will find that this is actually quite simple.

Samples and swatches

A professional interior designer relies heavily on swatches of fabric and tester pots of paint to put together and present a scheme — you should do the same. Whenever you see something that looks like it might be right, get a sample — as large as possible. Never be afraid to ask. Shops are sometimes rather tight with their samples and only offer the smallest snippet of fabric when you need to be able to see the complete pattern and all the colours it incorporates. If they aren't helpful, buy a small piece instead. Most paint manufacturers offer small sample pots of colour — if not, you will have to buy the smallest tin they sell.

Keep your samples together and always note down the manufacturer, the design name and any reference number so that you have them to hand for ordering. It will be useful if you also note down the price, the name of the shop and the fabric width and pattern repeat — so you can work out how much you will need and the final cost for your budget book. These notes will be useful too if you need to replace anything at a later date.

Keep these samples in a small bag, so that you can take them with you when you shop and make on-the-spot decisions about whether a fabric is going to work. Not many people can accurately carry colours in their head.

Facts and figures

Measurements are also hard to keep in your head. To rule out something on the spot for being too expensive, you have to know how much of it you need. Keep a note of all your various measurements (floor area for carpeting, wall area for wallpaper and window sizes for curtains and blinds) and carry it around with you at all times.

It is also useful to have a plan of your living room incorporating all these measurements. Put aside time to take detailed measurements of the room — ideally at the early planning stages. It is easy to forget some, so draw little sketches of each wall area (elevation) and mark on it every measurement, from the depth of the skirting to the width of the window frames. You don't need to be artistic, it is just a matter of using a pencil and ruler.

If you do a decent plan you can trace it on to sheets of tracing paper and experiment with different design ideas using coloured pens and pencils to colour walls, add mirrors, sketch window treatments and so on.

Do a floor plan too and mark on it where your existing power points are, where the radiator is and which way the door opens. All these points are vital, especially when it comes to choosing the furniture.

A question of balance

Design mistakes are often the result of an inability to imagine what a particular wallpaper will look like once it is on the wall

look like once it is on the wall and how the sofa or curtains will look next to it. Once the wallpaper is up or the fabric has been ordered, it is too late and too costly to change your mind. Spend some time now playing with your samples to gain an accurate impression (or as accurate as possible) of what the final effect will be.

Take your samples to the living room and position them in the spaces they are intended for. Tack a length of wallpaper to the wall, or paint some lining paper with your paint tester and tack that up. Put your carpet sample on the floor and your fabric samples on the sofa, armchair, window or wherever they will be. Keep them there for a week, not-

ing how they look under natural and artificial lights and at different times of day — especially at the times that you use your living room most.

Making a sample board

Next you need to get a picture of how the samples work together and try to achieve a good balance

of colour, pattern and texture. You can do this by making a sample board.

Use a piece of card as your base and think of it as your complete living room, or as a corner of the room where all your furnishing samples come together, such as by a window. The most visible expanses of colour or pattern will usually be the floor and walls, so cover the board with samples of those materials according to their relative space allocation in the room. The next largest samples are likely to be your sofa material and your curtains, so cut or fold these samples to an appropriate size in proportion to the walls and floor. Continue to position the samples of fabric as they would appear in the room, adjacent to and overlapping one another, until you have built up a picture of how the living room will look. If you can't get a sample for something (such as a lampshade), or if it is too heavy to position on a board (such as a floor tile), then use matching paint colours on the board instead.

Once the board is finished, appraise it critically. Does it look as you wanted or expected it to? Do the samples work together? Play around with them until you are happy with the overall look. Your sample board can turn into a work of art in its own right!

Ready to order
Check these points first:

● Are the fabrics suitable for your purposes (curtains, upholstery, etc)?
● Do they meet fire retardancy regulations?
● How washable are they? Can they be dry cleaned?
● Are all your wallpaper rolls of the same batch number? Order a spare roll for future patching.

Project one

Making a pelmet with a shaped edge

You will need:

- A spirit level and pencil
- Heavy-duty buckram
- Paper for a template
- Sharp scissors
- Lining or wadding fabric
- Top fabric
- PVA glue
- Velcro
- Board
- Brackets
- Screws

Pelmets add an extra dimension to a window dressing — and are very easy to make, using simple DIY skills. Think carefully about the scale of your pelmet before you begin. It shouldn't be too imposing or block out too much light in the room.

1 Decide on the depth and shape of your pelmet. It should look big enough to suit the length of your window and complement the style too. As a guide, it should also be roughly 15 cm (6 in) wider in total than the width of the window recess. Draw the shape you want onto a paper template first and fix it on the wall temporarily to see how it will look. Remember to make it long enough to turn back towards the wall at the sides if it is to fit around a pelmet board (see step 4).

39

4 Cut your board to the right length for your window and wide enough to allow a blind or curtain track to fit behind it, then fix it to the wall with angle brackets.

5 Stick the velcro along the sides and length of the pelmet board and either stick or stitch matching lengths of velcro to the wrong side of your fabric. Attach the pelmet to the board.

2 Using the paper template as a guide, cut out your shaped pelmet from pelmet buckram. Cut the lining or wadding fabric and final fabric using the same template, allowing an extra 3 cm (1¼ in) all round.

3 Lay the buckram flat and hold it down with weights while you cover it with the lining fabric or wadding. Make small snips into the edges of the fabric so that it can be folded over the shaped edges of the buckram neatly and stuck down with glue. Repeat the process with the top fabric, making sure that the fabric is pulled quite tight so that it lies smooth and free of wrinkles. Use pegs to keep it in place while you stick it to the pelmet.

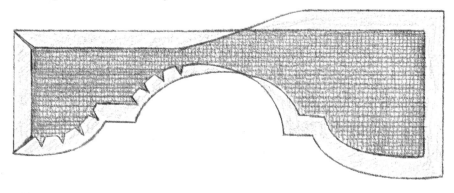

Variation

If your pelmet doesn't need to stand away from the wall, you can omit the pelmet board and simply stick a fabric pelmet directly to the wall. Cut strips of velcro, one just shorter than the length of the pelmet, and two smaller ones to support the sides of the pelmet. Now cut another three strips exactly the same. Stick the first three strips in place on the wall and either stick or stitch the other three to the pelmet itself. Finally, position the pelmet carefully on the wall.

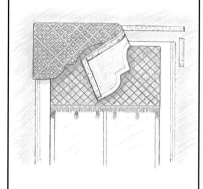

Variation

For a grander, more opulent look, combine your pelmet with a full, more dramatic curtain. If it's a false curtain, there purely for effect, why not cheat with your curtain heading and simply staple the fabric to a board concealed behind the pelmet.

Project two

Painted panels

You can add interest to a large expanse of wall by creating fake 'panels' simply with paint. Use painted panels to make a feature of a picture or collection, to give added depth to a small window frame or even to decorate a flat plain door. Once you get hooked on the idea, you may want to experiment with panels made from wallpaper borders to achieve an even more decorative look.

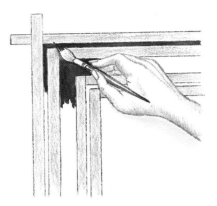

You will need:

- Plenty of masking tape
- Spirit level or plumb-line
- A pencil and straight edge
- Paint in a contrasting colour to your main wall
- A fine paint-brush for touching up
- Paint in your main wall colour, in case touching up is needed

1 Decide where you would like the panels to be and mark them out carefully using a pencil, a long straight edge as a guide and a spirit level and/or plumb-line. You will need

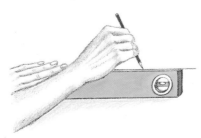

to draw two lines for each panel line to indicate the width of the finished painted line.

2 Stick masking tape down the outside of each drawn line to protect the surrounding wall. Take care to form sharp corners. Here both thick and thin lines have been used so you will have some strips of masking tape close together and others wider apart.

3 Paint between the tram lines formed by the masking tape in a contrasting colour to the main walls. Wait for the paint to dry, although not completely. Ideally the wall should be dry enough to remove the masking

tape without smudging the paint, but not so dry that the paint dries and cracks over the joins.

4 Remove the masking tape carefully to reveal the painted panels. Be prepared for the masking tape to remove some of the old paintwork and have some of that paint and a fine brush on hand for touching up once the paint has dried completely.

Variation

The same technique can be used for creating a fake dado rail — it's cheaper and more interesting than the real thing.

- Draw a straight line running parallel to the floor at about the height of a chair back.
- Create a dado with masking tape and then paint between the guides.
- For best effect use three paint colours — one for the dado itself and two different ones for above and below it.

Project three
Shelving

Even if you lack the confidence to knock a nail into the wall, you can create useful and stylish shelving. Why restrict yourself to boring brackets when with a little imagination you can build shelves from almost anything sturdy enough to bear some weight?

Here storage pots, small chests of drawers and wine racks all take the strain — making your shelves work doubly hard for you by offering extra storage space into the bargain.

Right: Perfect for the home office, these basic chests of drawers were given a quick wash of colour then set to use storing staples and other small items.

Left: Glass storage jars can be filled with anything from pebbles or coloured stones to brightly wrapped sweets (if you think you can resist them) to create quirky, decorative shelving supports.

Above: Simple wine racks make perfect shelving supports for the dining
room or kitchen, and, luckily, they
look as effective empty as they do
when they're full!

Project four
Making curtain tie-backs

It is surprisingly easy and rewarding to make these tie-backs and chunky tassels, using colours that match your curtains perfectly. You will need a friend to help, so it is a sociable task too!

You will need:

- Two paper or polystyrene craft balls, for the balls at the top of the tassel
- 100 g (3½ oz) chunky cotton chenille in one or two colours
- Linen carpet thread
- Sharp-pointed scissors
- A large tapestry needle
- A piece of thick card
- Sharp scissors

1 Using the tip of your scissors, hollow out the craft ball as if you were decoring an apple until the hole is half the size of the ball. Trim any rough edges with nail scissors.

2 To make a tassel ball: thread a generous amount of cotton through the tapestry needle and knot one end. Take the needle through the middle of the ball and pass the cotton through the knot to secure it. Hide the knot on the inside of the ball and continue to pass the needle through the centre hole until the ball is covered with a single, smooth layer. Once this is done, finish off the end of the cotton inside the ball. If you want to use two colours, leave spaces in between the threads of the first

colour and then wind the second colour within them.

3 To make the tassel: Decide how long you would like your tassel tail to be. Cut a piece of stiff card so that it is about 12 cm (4¾ in) wide, and the depth of the tassel plus a little. Using the cotton straight from the ball, wind it around the card until it looks thick enough for the tassel. If you want to use two colours, wind them around the card together so that they are evenly distributed.

4 Secure the tassel by winding a piece of linen thread twice through the top of the cotton and tying it.

5 Cut the cotton evenly at the other end of the card and remove card. Trim the tail neatly.

6 To make two-coloured rope cord (you need a friend for this bit): take three 140 cm (56 in) lengths of one colour of cotton, fold them in half and knot the free ends together. Repeat with three strands of the other colour. Give one knot to your friend to hold and the other knot to yourself. Tie the two folded ends together to make a knot halfway between the two of you.

7 The two of you then have to twist each end in a clockwise direction until the cotton is quite tight and begins to get a bit curly. Take hold of the centre knot and bring the outer knots, which you have been twisting,

together. Tie the free ends together, holding on tightly to the centre knot — the cord will twirl up as soon as you let go of it. Run your hand down the cord to even out the twists.

8 Fold the rope cord in half and push the looped end through your cotton-covered ball. Sew the other two loose ends to the tassel with your linen thread, then pull the ball down over the join and tidy up the tassel bottom again.

9 To make rope cord for the tie-back: this is made in the same way as the slim rope cord, but using eight 3 m (3 yd) pieces of both yarns (16 lengths of 3 m). You need to measure out and hold the lengths very carefully as it is easy to get such long lengths tied and muddled.

Project five

Making and using a rubber stamp

Making your own stamp is far more satisfying than using a manufactured one, and, if you pick out a design or motif used in the pattern on your curtains or soft furnishings, you can create a real designer finish. A rubber stamp is a very versatile decorative device which can be used on walls, furniture, floors and fabrics.

You will need:
- Carbon paper
- A sheet of rubber
- Foam
- Wooden block
- Craft knife
- Artists' acrylic paint or paint blocks

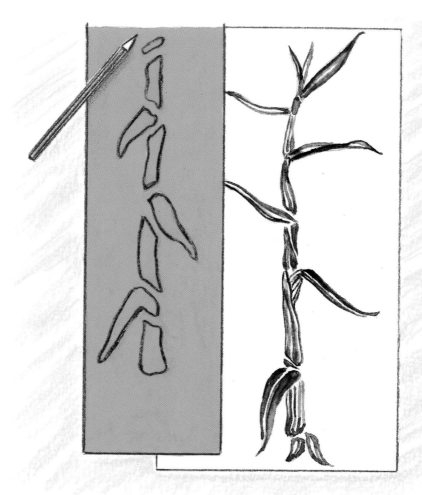

1 Transfer the design on to the rubber which will form the top of your stamp. Carbon paper is useful for tracing the design from a cut-off of the fabric, or you can cut out the design and draw round it.

The bamboo design shown here was adapted slightly to make it narrower for use on the mirror frame — the stem was copied and then the leaves were adapted.

5 Paint the mirror frame carefully with at least two coats of good-quality wood paint over a coat of primer. Rub each coat gently with fine sandpaper when it is dry to ensure a smooth surface. Leave to dry completely.

6 Using chalk or water-based crayons, mark on the item where you will position the stamp once it is loaded with paint. Use artists' acrylic paint straight from the tube or paint blocks, which are available from stamp suppliers (these dry slowly on a painted surface so use artists' acrylics if you want to put the item to use quickly). Dab paint onto your stamp evenly using a chunk of smooth sponge. Cover the whole design evenly.

2 Glue a piece of the foam to your wooden block and carefully cut out your design in rubber using sharp scissors or a craft knife. You can be fairly economical with the foam — it does not need to be in one section as it will be behind the stamping surface. Stick the cut-out pieces of your stamp to the foam and press them firmly into place.

3 Test your stamp on a piece of paper before using it. This is how your stamp will look every time you print it, so make any changes now.

4 Cut away the excess backing foam with a craft knife. This is important as your stamp design needs to stand proud of the wooden block in order to prevent excess paint from transferring on to your work when you apply pressure and rock the stamp.

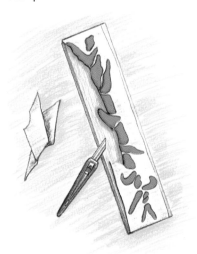

7 Position the stamp where you have marked, taking care not to touch it on to the painted surface until you are sure that it is correctly placed. Using two hands, press the stamp firmly into place and rock it very gently. Lift the stamp upwards, taking care not to smudge it. Any runs of paint can be removed immediately with a cotton bud.

8 When the mirror frame is dry, protect it with a coat of varnish.

Project six

Decorating frames

Personalize picture and mirror frames by decorating them with simple painted designs. Search out paint colours which complement those in your living-room scheme — or you could take your inspiration from fabric already in the room.

Frames always look better when hung in groups, so why not decorate several using the same design but different shades of paint?

You will need:
- Paint or varnish remover (if the frame is already decorated)
- Wood primer
- Wet-and-dry sandpaper
- Eggshell for the base coat
- Artists' acrylic paint for the decorative finish
- Clear non-yellowing polyurethane varnish
- A pencil and fine paint-brush for decorating
- A brush for applying the base coat
- A brush for the varnish

1 Prepare your frame by removing old varnish or peeling paint, and sanding the surface. If for any reason you cannot remove the mirror or picture within the frame, protect it well with masking tape.

2 Apply a wood primer to seal the frame. This will prevent further coats of paint from soaking into the wood.

3 Paint on your eggshell base coat. Eggshell is harder wearing than emulsion and has a slight sheen. These frames have been painted in an off-white colour, such as magnolia. Leave the frames to dry. You may need to apply more than one coat of this, in which case sand the frame carefully between each coat with a wet-and-dry sandpaper for a smooth finish.

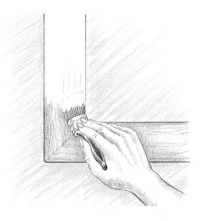

4 Use a pencil to trace on your surface design if you are not confident of your freehand skills and practise on paper first.

5 Use a fine paint-brush and acrylic paint to decorate the frame. Let the frame dry after you use each colour to avoid the colours smudging and mixing. On these frames only one colour was used,

but you can see how the paint smudged slightly where the lines crossed each other.

6 To finish and protect the frame, use a non-yellowing clear varnish. Do not worry if the varnish looks off-white or honey-coloured in the tin — it will dry with a clear finish.

Project seven

Distressing furniture

Give an old piece of furniture a new lease of life by making it fashionably 'distressed'. It is easy to do and the effect can be stunning — you can even achieve the same look with a new piece of furniture.

1 Prepare your furniture by first making sure it is sound. Repair any damage. Remove old paint and varnish and sand down ready for painting.

2 Decide what colours you want to use. This chest has been distressed to reveal bare wood beneath the paint, but you could equally paint your chest with a base colour that will show through when you distress the top coat. You could even use three colours.

3 Paint the chest with your first (or only) coat of paint, which should be a water-based emulsion, and leave it to dry thoroughly. If you want to reveal bare wood when you distress the chest, go straight to the next step. If not, paint another colour on top of the first.

4 Use sandpaper to work at the paint surface in the areas you want to distress, moving in the direction of the grain. For a truly authentic look distress only the places that would have received most wear, such as the handles and surrounding areas.

5 For a more distressed look, use a wire brush or coarse wire wool to remove the paint — you could even scratch the chest with a bunch of keys and blunt the corners and add a few dents with a round-headed hammer.

6 If you want to protect the look you have created, coat it in matt polyurethane varnish. Otherwise, leave it bare to allow the distressing process to continue naturally!

Project eight
Painted floors

V arnished floorboards are attractive, but a painted floor can be a real showpiece. The art is not in the painting, but in the planning and preparation .....

You will need:
- 3 tins of eggshell paint
- White spirit
- Cloth
- Low-tack masking tape
- Straight edge for marking out pattern
- Pencil and rubber
- Decorators' paint-brush
- Non-yellowing oil-based varnish

1 Prepare the wood for painting. If the floor is bare new wood, seal any knots with knotting solution, sand lightly and prime with wood primer. If the floorboards are already varnished or painted, sand them down to provide a key for the new coat of paint.

2 Apply a base coat of eggshell paint in the lightest shade of the colours to be used (in this case minty cream). Paint the entire area. Leave to dry overnight.

3 Plan your design to scale on squared paper and then measure and mark out the design in pencil on the floor.

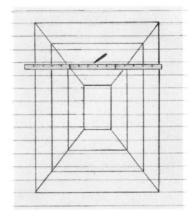

4 Using low-tack masking tape, outline the areas of the design where the second colour (in this case

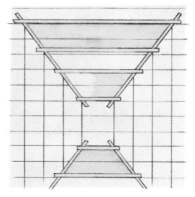

pale green) is to be applied and then paint in these sections. Leave to dry before removing the masking tape. If two coats are needed to achieve a strong opaque colour, leave the first coat to dry overnight. If any runs have crept under the tape, they can be wiped off at this stage with a cloth dabbed in white spirit.

5 Mask off the areas of the design where the third colour (in this case the darker green) is to be applied and then paint in these sections. Leave to dry before removing the masking tape.

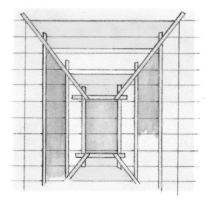

6 For extra protection (especially for light colours) apply two or more coats of a non-yellowing oil-based varnish. Dead-flat matt varnish has been used here.

Project nine

Decorating lampshades

Bring dull lampshades to life with your own unique design. Why settle for lampshades that will merely 'do', when, with a little imagination, you can create shades that will complement and enhance your living-room scheme? Here I have used a simple stencil and a stamp to create two quite different looks.

You will need
- A lampshade which is made of stiff fabric that will take paint, and is not too curved
- A stamp
- A small roller or sponge
- A tray or dish for paint

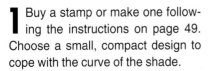

1 Buy a stamp or make one following the instructions on page 49. Choose a small, compact design to cope with the curve of the shade.

2 Pour a little paint onto a sheet of glass or a plate and use a roller or small sponge to coat the stamp evenly. I used special stamping paint, suitable for use on fabrics. Practise using the stamp on a piece of spare fabric or ideally on an old lampshade that you no longer want.

3 Hold the lampshade in such a way that it doesn't bend under the pressure of the stamp, and gently but firmly press the stamp onto it. Repeat around the shade, always re-coating the stamp with paint before applying it to the shade. Work away from the stamp you have just made so that you don't smudge the paint.

Variation: Stencilling a shade
- Again, choose or make a stencil which suits the curve and size of the lampshade. Using fabric or stencil paint and a stencil brush, hold the stencil firmly against the shade and stipple in the paint. Practise on something first to find the best way of achieving the effect you want. Repeat the design around the shade, working away from the stencil you have just done so you do not smudge the paint.

Project ten
Sofa throwover

By making your own throw you not only guarantee that it will fit your sofa properly, but you also have more choice when it comes to fabrics — you could even make up some extra cushion covers from the same material to unite the colour scheme around the room. A successful throw is cut generously so that it does not slip off whenever anyone sits on the sofa. It will drive you mad if you are forever adjusting it. Press the throw after you've finished sewing and then play around with its position on the sofa to achieve the best look.

You will need:
- A measuring tape
- Enough material to cover your sofa generously (see Step 1)
- Binding tape in a contrasting colour
- Matching thread and thread for tacking
- Needles and pins

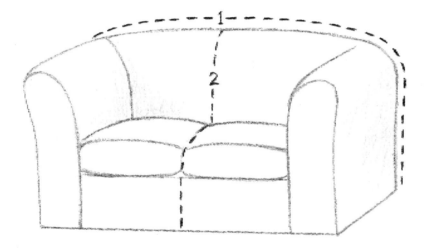

1 To estimate the amount of fabric you need, measure your sofa from floor to arm up the back, along the back and down over the arm to the floor again. Add on your pattern repeat plus 15 cm (6 in) for working (measurement 1, the width you need). Then measure from the floor at the back, up the back and over the top, down back across the seat and down to the floor. Add on your pattern repeat plus 15 cm (6 in) for working (measurement 2, the length you need). As fabric comes in fairly narrow widths, you will find you need to work with at least two widths of your fabric.

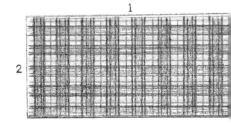

2 French seam your widths of fabric together to create a hardwearing join. This is done by placing the fabric wrong sides together and, with the pattern matching, pinning along the final join line. Tack along 12 mm (½ in) from the pin line with your raw edges level, then machine stitch along the tacking.

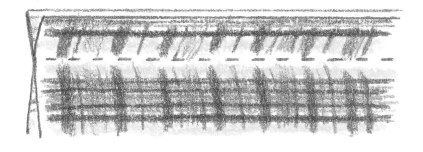

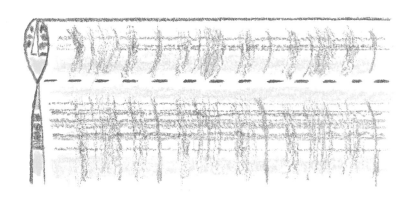

3 Trim the seam to 3 mm (⅛ in). Remove the pins, and press the seams open. Tack 6 mm (¼ in) from the first seam with your fabric folded right sides together, check the pattern match, and stitch along the tacking. Press the seam with the allowance to one side.

4 Estimate the amount of binding needed by measuring round all the edges of the throwover, plus 15 cm (6 in) for working. Press the binding off centre then place it with the larger overlap on the wrong side of the fabric, and tack into place. When placing the binding to the corners, mitre the corners for a neat finish by folding the corners diagonally, trimming them off, then folding both edges in place before slip stitching the diagonal seam. Machine stitch along the tacking.

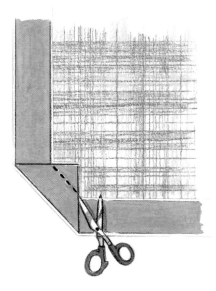

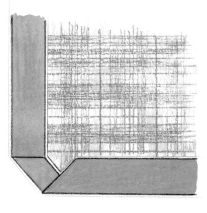

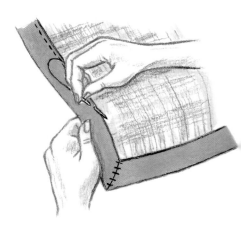

Suppliers

Crucial Trading
77 Westbourne Park Road
London W2
Tel: 0171 221 9000
Sofa Throwover – page 60

Elephant
94 Tottenham Court Road
London W1
Tel: 0171 813 2092
Shelving – page 44
Sofa Throwover – page 60

Nice Irma's
46 Goodge Street
London W1
Tel: 0171 580 6921
Shelving – page 44
Painted Floors – page 56
Sofa Throwover – page 60

Oliver Bonas
801 Fulham Road
London SW6
Tel: 0171 736 8435
Shelving – page 44
Sofa Throwover – page 60

Paperchase
213 Tottenham Court Road
London W1
Tel: 0171 580 8496
Shelving – page 44

The Pier
200 Tottenham Court Road
London W1
Tel: 0171 637 7001
Shelving – page 44
Painted Floors – page 56
Sofa Throwover – page 60

Index